WEALTH & JUSTICE
THE MORALITY OF DEMOCRATIC CAPITALISM

WEALTH & JUSTICE
THE MORALITY OF DEMOCRATIC CAPITALISM

Peter Wehner & Arthur C. Brooks

AEI Press
Publisher for the American Enterprise Institute
Washington, D.C.

Distributed by arrangement with the National Book Network
15200 NBN Way, Blue Ridge Summit, PA 17214
To order call toll free 1-800-462-6420 or 1-717-794-3800.

For all other inquiries please contact AEI Press, 1150 17th Street, N.W.,
Washington, D.C. 20036 or call 1-800-862-5801.

Cover Design by Amy Duty and Justin Mezzell
Interior design by Amy Duty, Justin Mezzell, and Jesse Penico

LCCN: 2010028987
ISBN-13: ISBN-13: 978-0-8447-4377-6
eISBN-13: ISBN-13: 978-0-8447-4378-3

CONTENTS

FOREWORD
Philip Jenkins

A French intellectual is said to have dismissed a scheme in scornful terms: "Well, yes," he sniffed, "of course the idea works well in practice. But I'm afraid it just doesn't work in *theory*." That remark neatly summarizes a common response to capitalism, the economic system that shapes virtually everything we do, that has created such incalculable prosperity, and that is the basis of our political freedom. Yet, for all its wonders, even well educated people often find it very difficult to justify the philosophical or moral assumptions underpinning that system.

Indeed, it is all too easy to damn capitalism in moral terms. Capitalism, we hear, is synonymous with greed and selfishness; it is founded on human exploitation; it violates religious injunctions against materialism and covetousness. A familiar leftist slogan poses a critical choice between "socialism or barbarism." So successful has such scathing rhetoric been through the decades that even proud advocates of capitalism are nervous about using the word, preferring to speak of the "free enterprise system," or just "the market." Capitalism is the triumphant success story that dare not speak its name.

That is the problem that Peter Wehner and Arthur C. Brooks seek to remedy in *Wealth and Justice: The Morality of Democratic Capitalism*, and they succeed impressively. The book takes sophisticated arguments from economics and philosophy and makes them available in terms accessible to the ordinary person. Not only does capitalism have a moral basis, the authors show, but it is absolutely founded in a particular anthropology, a view of human nature, which is also that of America's founding fathers. Like other great Enlightenment thinkers, the founders knew that human beings were neither angels nor demons; they were not hopelessly corrupt, but neither were they perfectible. Human beings were driven by rational self-interest, which ultimately could benefit both themselves and the wider society. Wehner and Brooks show just how sizable these benefits could be. The vast historical achievements of the capitalist system are overwhelmingly greater than that of any rival economic order or theory. In fact, whenever other social systems have come close to matching the capitalist record, they have done so by adopting capitalist methods, without accepting the capitalist title.

But what about the moral critique? It is here that Wehner and Brooks make their greatest contribution to public discourse, and most convincingly challenge popular wisdom. Above all, they show that advocacy of capitalism is thoroughly grounded in morality, and arguably far more so than are rival creeds, such as socialism. If morality means pursuing the common good, then capitalism is an impeccably moral system.

While I will take away many insights from *Wealth and Justice*, I find particularly rewarding Wehner and Brooks' demolition of the argument that economics is a zero-sum game, a struggle for fixed resources in which the poor inevitably confront the rich. In the United States, as in most Western countries, many well intentioned people believe that the economy can be compared to a cake of a fixed size, so that some people have a bigger share than others. The only real political question is how that cake should be distributed. If it is neither just nor reasonable that some people should have more than others, then the cake must be redistributed by means of taxation and official policies, to be undertaken by an intrusive activist state. The resulting constraints on personal freedom may be regrettable, but morality and religion demand such a course. Americans call these policies "progressive," suggesting that they push society in the inevitable direction favored by history. In the progressive vision, anyone who opposes such an approach must be acting from motives of greed and unreasonable self-interest—that is, they must be running flat contrary to morality and justice.

Missing from such a vision is the fundamental historical fact that the "cake" is not fixed in size. Capitalism produces ever more wealth, which tends inexorably to benefit all members of the community. The dissemination of wealth does not, of course, occur at the same rate among all sections of the population, or to the same degree, but it ultimately does benefit everyone, and far more efficiently than can be accomplished by state mechanisms. This process will occur unless the natural workings of capitalism are sabotaged by ill-judged social interventions, which ultimately offer their chief benefits to bureaucrats and political elites. In the most extreme circumstances, interventionist states shed their benevolent masks and become nightmarish tyrannies. As the familiar maxim declares, a government that can do everything *for* you can also do anything it wants *to* you. n terms of their record of improving the lot of ordinary people, "progressive" policies are sadly misnamed. Not only can capitalism be reconciled with religion and morality, it is also the natural outcome of our most deeply held principles.

Wehner and Brooks present a very rich argument, which is all the more provocative for being presented in such a short space. But when we expand these arguments, when we test them against known historical experience, we find ever more illustrations that prove their case.

In fact, the best argument we can ever make for capitalism and its accomplishments is this: Just imagine the world without it. It's not hard to do. Just ask a historian of virtually any society that existed across the globe prior to the capitalist expansion of the eighteenth century. By our contemporary standards, those societies were unimaginably poor, and not just in the sense that they lacked frivolous modern luxuries. Life was a constant struggle for food and resources, while production depended on the number of human beings that elites could dragoon into the labor force. What was society like before capitalism? I borrow the phrase of historian Eugen Weber: It was a world of scarcity, stagnation, servitude, superstition, and sharp stratification. Only a fool would view that "world we have lost" with the slightest nostalgia.

But capitalism brought abundance. It made available to millions of ordinary people access to goods, services, and leisure on a scale not available to the very richest in pre-modern times. And from that abundance stemmed blessings that were the exact inverse of the curses named by Weber. Abundance brought growth and progress, liberation, science and education, and democracy. And that democracy gradually expanded to comprehend categories wholly excluded from the old political order, most strikingly for women.

The capitalist revolution also brought these blessings to a wider and vaster world. The whole human population in 1800 was around 1 billion, rising to 1.6 billion in 1900, and 6.5 billion today. Capitalism has not only made it possible for the globe to support that vast increase, it has also greatly raised the living standards of those additional people, and immeasurably expanded their opportunities. Just since 1980, the number of people that capitalism has raised from absolute poverty is significantly larger than the total population of the world in the era of Napoleon and Thomas Jefferson. Whenever I see wealthy Americans and Europeans demonstrating against "globalization" and capitalism, I often think that we mislabel those terms. Rather than anti-globalization, let us give their cause its true name: pro-poverty.

Yet, so many of us take these miracles for granted. On more than one occasion, I have heard scholars—well educated and widely traveled individuals—denounce the horrors of consumerism and materialism, that dreadful world that the profit motive has created. We don't need all these material goods, they tell us. Capitalism just drives us to want more and more; it feeds our lust for possessions. We should resist the blandishments of consumerism, and only use those basic goods that we absolutely need for a comfortable life. Resist capitalism!

But then you start asking: So what are those basic, essential goods and services that we all agree we need, and which can be separated from meaningless luxuries? In most cases, the answer is simple: Those goods that activists define as essential are what they regarded as natural and universal when they were young adults, so that everything that came along later is consumerist vanity. So, bicycles and cars are essential, as are electrical power and heating, ovens and washing machines, antibiotics and disinfectants. Presumably, in twenty years, when anti-consumerist critics are denouncing unnecessary luxuries, they will not include such fundamental necessities as computers and PDAs, MP3 players and video game consoles. In forty years, the list of basic old-fashioned necessities will certainly include devices and services that have not even been invented as of 2010.

In other words, capitalism constantly expands and enhances the material goods that we rely on, things that make our lives more comfortable and efficient, and it does this so rapidly that most of us are barely aware of the constant state of transformation. An anti-capitalist critic might object that the system is thus creating ever more numerous artificial wants and desires, inventing ever more goods that we cannot do without. It would be truer to say that capitalism is constantly expanding the spectrum of human capacities, broadening and deepening the range of human experience, and offering those new insights and techniques on a global scale. Capitalism liberates; that is its nature.

And I do stress that we are dealing with *capitalism*, rather than more generally science, technology, or invention. Through human history, many different societies have made daring scientific leaps, and so many inventions that we think of as modern in fact have ancient precedents. Just look, for instance, at the Antikythera mechanism, a bizarre object discovered in a Mediterranean shipwreck, which proved to date to around 150 BCE. Only recently have we been able to show that this 2,000 year-old object was in fact a dazzlingly efficient mechanical computer designed to trace astronomical patterns. In the first century CE, Hero of Alexandria described a working model of a steam-powered device, his *aeolipyle*. Through the centuries, different societies—Chinese, Indian, Arab—produced comparable wonders. But these potential breakthroughs remained the preserve of scholars and elites, rather than serving as the basis for mass social and cultural change. They were deluxe toys, not world-historical game-changers.

Invention can only change the world when it is combined with the correct social and economic mechanisms that allow the cultivation of rational self-interest. Again, these are things that we take for granted, but they would have amazed earlier ages. Above all, a society needs a well-defined concept of property, so that ideas and innovations are the unquestioned possession of a particular individual or family, and cannot simply be appropriated at the whim of some larcenous lord. Property is the basis of prosperity, and it must be reaffirmed by known and sacrosanct rights of inheritance, defended by neutral courts. Only then is there the slightest incentive for an entrepreneur to invest in developing an idea, to make it marketable—to provide the basis for capitalism. Thus, the Industrial Revolution based upon the steam engine simply could not take off in the first century, but had to wait some 1,700 years for the work of James Watt and—no less important—his financial backers. The era of practical computing had to wait even longer.

As economists like Hernando de Soto have argued, the greatest single problem facing hundreds of millions of poor people worldwide is the lack of legal property rights. As they do not even have rights to homes they might have lived in for generations, they are not able to use equity to raise loans or mortgages, and thereby improve their position. Without rights of property and inheritance, vast sectors of humanity are doomed to pauperism, to the myriad dysfunctions that we label with the despairing term "Third World."

Again, the best way to understand the meaning of capitalism is to examine a society lacking its principles, and we need not travel to Africa or Asia to do that. Many of us remember the cultural and economic devastation that prevailed on American Indian reservations through the twentieth century, those landscapes of battered trailers, a society torn apart by alcoholism and domestic violence. Yet, by nature, the people forced to live in those conditions were as hardworking, creative, thoughtful, and resilient as any on the planet—and, incidentally, they had ancient commercial traditions. What had gone wrong was the lack of property rights, decreed by a U.S. government dazzled by nostalgic visions of communal societies free of greed or exploitation, free (in short) of the curse of capitalism. The practical consequence of this well-meant tyranny was that no individual could acquire or sell reservation property, and thus could not raise loans; hence the trailers, which banks could remove if and when foreclosure became necessary. Government would supply all needs—which it did in the miserly and incompetent way that we expect from officialdom. Indians thus suffered both socialism and barbarism, inflicted from above. Lacking any chance of improvement or prosperity, communities declined into hopeless nihilism. Few examples better illustrate the intimate link between economic stagnation and moral disintegration. Capitalism is indeed a moral issue.

It is also a matter of religion. As I suggested earlier, critics of capitalism have been highly successful in claiming the religious high ground, using familiar Judaeo-Christian scriptures to condemn greed and materialism. But, as *Wealth and Justice* shows clearly, advocates of capitalism also have excellent arguments, which deserve to be better known.

Wehner and Brooks aptly quote Jim Wallis, editor of the magazine *Sojourners* and one of the most articulate left-wing voices in evangelical Christianity today. Wallis points out that if you remove every reference to "the poor" from the Bible, you are left with quite a thin tract, and he is undoubtedly right. The prophets of ancient Israel made the care and protection of the poor a fundamental value, and excoriated any forms of ritual piety that failed to take account of their interest. Early Christianity likewise identified strongly with the cause not just of the poor but also of the absolutely downtrodden, *hoi ptochoi*. But how exactly should one help the poor? For Wallis, the answer lies in state intervention and socialist policies of wealth redistribution, but there is no reason to suppose that the Bible demands such policies, especially when they so frequently clash with other fundamental values, including the centrality of family. Historical experience leaves not the slightest doubt of the superiority of free-enterprise capitalism as the best means of helping the poor—or rather, of making them self sufficient, so that they no longer need help. Of course, as Wehner and Brooks write, no earthly system is perfect, and capitalism has its litany of horror stories. But, in terms of effectiveness, in terms of fulfilling the Biblical mission to raise the poor, the system has no equal.

The Bible offers no one formula for social or economic organization, and reading selectively, you can find scriptural warrant for almost any "-ism" you care to name (provided you acknowledge that indispensable core of concern for the poor). But some Biblical themes are perennial, and one of the most prominent is that of individual responsibility. Of course, the Bible acknowledges the role of family and society, but it also recognizes that ultimately, you make your own decisions, and stand by them. You shape your own fate, in this world and the next. In the sixth century BCE, the prophet Ezekiel quoted the old proverb: "The fathers have eaten sour grapes, and the children's teeth are set on edge" (Ezekiel 18:2), but he cites the words only in order to repeal them. Henceforth, says God, that proverb no longer applies. Once upon a time, guilt was a collective matter, and the sin of one person reverberated through his family or clan. Now, though, that principle is no longer valid: "The soul who sins is the one who will die" (Jeremiah 31:29). The prophet Jeremiah spoke similar words, and the underlying ideas echo through the New Testament.

So obvious is this idea of individual responsibility, so fundamental to everything we believe, that we scarcely recognize its radicalism in the ancient world. But it was, and remains, a revolutionary theory, with profound consequences for our understanding of human behavior, our anthropology. And, as Wehner and Brooks show, this concept of human nature is what ultimately fires economic progress. If you are looking for a Biblical basis for the anthropology of capitalism, you can indeed find it.

I concentrate on these Biblical themes because they carry special weight in the contemporary world. We live, after all, in an age of epochal religious change, as Christianity has spread so rapidly across the global South, most tellingly in Africa and Asia, into traditionally poor regions that have proved impervious to each and every scheme for economic development. As Wehner and Brooks remark, Africa above all has earned a grim reputation as an economic basket case. But as I say, we live in exciting times. The number of Christians in Africa has grown from around 10 million in 1900—10 percent of the population—to perhaps 470 million today, or 46 percent, and some projections suggest that Africa will have 1 billion Christians by 2050. By that point, Africa will be home to by far the world's largest concentration of Christians.

Such a story is critical for scholars of Christianity, but some believe that it might also have wide ramifications for economic progress. While Christian churches vary enormously in their social ideologies, some of the most successful and fastest-growing denominations preach impressive messages of self-reliance, thrift, and individual responsibility, teachings that could well form the basis for new kinds of civil society. Totally committed to raising the poor, these churches know all too well that they must rely on their own efforts, rather than depending on government. Ideally, they could lay the foundations for a new economic order that would replace the catastrophic failures of statism. Conceivably, we stand at the threshold of yet another of capitalism's great eras of expansion, creating prosperity where all other means have failed.

If, in fact, religion supported an economic restructuring that rescued Africa from despair and immiseration, it would achieve one of the greatest and most beneficial revolutions in human history. But it would not be the first such achievement in history of capitalism, the economic system that created the world we know.

Although the debate over capitalism is critical for virtually all of our political life, the intellectual arguments on either side are poorly understood. Read *Wealth and Justice*, and prepare to be exposed to some exhilarating ideas.

CHAPTER I.
HUMAN NATURE AND CAPITALISM

At the core of every social, political, and economic system is a picture of human nature (to paraphrase the twentieth-century columnist Walter Lippmann). The suppositions we begin with—the ways in which that picture is developed—determine the lives we lead, the institutions we build, and the civilizations we create. They are the foundation stone.

THREE VIEWS OF HUMAN NATURE

During the eighteenth century—a period that saw the advent of modern capitalism—there were several different currents of thought about the nature of the human person. Three models were particularly significant.

One model was that humans, while flawed, are perfectible. A second was that we are flawed and fatally so; we need to accept and build our society around this unpleasant reality. A third view was that although human beings are flawed, we are capable of virtuous acts and self-government—that under the right circumstances, human nature can work to the advantage of the whole.

The first school included those who (representing the French Enlightenment) believed in the perfectibility of man and the pre-eminence of scientific rationalism. Their plans were grandiose, utopian, revolutionary, and aimed at "the universal regeneration of mankind" and the creation of a "New Man."[1]

Such notions, espoused by Jean-Jacques Rousseau and other Enlightenment *philosophes*, heavily influenced a later generation of socialist thinkers. These theorists—Robert Owen, Charles Fourier, and Henri de Saint-Simon among them—believed that human nature was as easily reshaped as hot wax. Human nature was considered plastic and malleable, to the point that there was no fixed human nature to speak of; it could therefore be molded into anything the architects of a social system imagined.

These theorists dreamed of a communal society, liberated from private property and free of human inequality. They articulated a theory of human nature and socioeconomic org anization that eventually influenced capitalism's most famous and bitter critic, the German philosopher, economist, and revo lutionary Karl Marx.

The second current of thought, embodied in the writings of seventeenth-century Englishmen Thomas Hobbes and Bernard Mandeville, viewed human nature as more nearly the opposite:

inelastic, brittle, and unalterable. And people were, at their core, antisocial beings.

Hobbes, for example, worried that people were ever in danger of lapsing into a pre-civilized state, "without a common power to keep them all in awe," which, in turn, would lead to a hopeless existence, a "state of nature" characterized by "a war of every man, against every man." It was, Hobbes wrote, a life "solitary, poor, nasty, brutish, and short." To avoid this fate, we must submit to the authority of the state, what he termed the "Leviathan" (a monstrous, multi-headed sea creature mentioned in the Hebrew Bible). In the process, we would gain self-preservation, but it would come at the expense of liberty.[2]

The third model of human nature is found in the thinking of the American founders. "If men were angels," wrote James Madison, the father of the Constitution, in Federalist Paper No. 51, "no government would be necessary." But Madison and the other founders knew men were *not* angels and would never *become* angels. They believed instead that human nature was mixed, a combination of virtue and vice, nobility and corruption. People were swayed by both reason and passion, capable of self-government but not to be trusted with absolute power. The founders' assumption was that within every human heart, let alone among different individuals, were competing and sometimes contradictory moral impulses and currents.

This last view of human nature is consistent with and reflective of Christian teaching. The Scriptures teach that we are both made in the image of God and fallen creatures; in the words of Saint Paul, we can be "instruments of wickedness" as well as "instruments of righteousness."[3] All have sinned and fallen short of the glory of God, the Bible declares—yet it also tells us to be holy in all our conduct, to walk in His statutes, and not to grow weary in doing good. Human beings are capable of acts of squalor and acts of nobility; we can pursue vice and we can pursue virtue.

As for the matter of the state: Romans 13 makes clear that government is divinely sanctioned by God to preserve public order, to restrain evil, and to make justice possible. This, too, was a view shared by many of the founders. Government itself is a reflection of human nature, they argued, "because the passions of men will not conform to the dictates of reason and justice without constraint."[4]

The Anglo-Scottish Enlightenment philosophies of Adam Smith, David Hume, and Francis Hutcheson both informed and aligned with the views of the American founders and Christian teaching. Smith was himself a professor of moral philosophy; *The Theory of Moral Sentiments*[5] preceded *The Wealth of Nations.*[6] Smith and his compatriots did not believe in the perfectibility of human nature and thought it foolish to build any human institution on the possibility that such perfection could be attained. Neither did they believe that human nature was irredeemably corrupt and devoid of virtue.

SELF INTEREST: A POSITIVE OR NEGATIVE HUMAN CHARACTERISTIC?

The American founders believed, and capitalism rests on the belief, that people are driven by "self-interest" and the desire to better our condition. Self-interest is not necessarily a bad thing; in fact, Smith believed, and capitalism presupposes, that the general welfare depends on allowing an individual to pursue his self-interest "as long as he does not violate the laws of justice." When a person acts in his own interest, "he frequently promotes [the interest] of society more effectually than when he really intends to promote it.[7]"

Michel Guillaume Jean de Crèvecœur, among the first writers who attempted to explain the American frontier and the concept of the "American Dream" to a European audience, captured this view when he wrote:

> The American ought therefore to love this country much better than that wherein either he or his forefathers were born. Here the rewards of his industry follow with equal steps the progress of his labour; his labour is founded on the basis of nature, *self-interest*; can it want a stronger allurement?[8]

Smith took for granted that people are driven by self-interest, by the desire to better their condition. "It is not from the benevolence of the butcher, the brewer, or the baker that we expect our dinner," is how he put it, "but from their regard to their own interest. We address ourselves not to their humanity, but to their self-love, and never talk to them of our own necessities but of their advantages."[9]

Harnessed and channeled the right way, then, self-interest— when placed within certain rules and boundaries—can be a very good thing, leading to a more prosperous and humane society.

Here it's important to draw a distinction between *self-interest* and *selfishness*. Self-interest—unlike selfishness—will often lead one to commit acts of altruism; rightly understood, it knows that no man is an island, that we are part of a larger community, and that what is good for others is good for us. To put it another way: Pursuing our own good can advance the common good. Even more, advancing the common good can advance our own good, as every Christian knows full well.

Advocates of free enterprise believe that creativity, enterprise, and ingenuity are essential parts of human nature. Capitalism aims to take advantage of the self-interest of human nature, knowing that the collateral effects will be a more decent and benevolent society. Capitalists believe that liberty is an inherent good and should form the cornerstone not only of our political institutions but our economic ones as well. Free-market advocates also insist that wealth and prosperity can mitigate envy and resentment, which have acidic effects on human relations. Markets, precisely because they are wealth-generating, also end up being wealth-distributing.

THE RELATIONSHIP BETWEEN HUMAN NATURE
AND GOVERNMENT

Why does all of this matter? Because our "picture of human nature" determines in large measure the institutions we design. For example, the architects of our government carefully studied history and every conceivable political arrangement that had been devised up to their time. In the course of their analysis, they made fundamental judgments about human nature and designed a constitutional form of government with it in mind.

What is true for the creation of political institutions is also true for economic ones. They, too, proceed from an understanding of human behavior.

It is hard to overstate the importance of this matter. The model of human nature one espouses will guide and shape everything else, from the economic system one embraces (free-market capitalism versus socialism) to the political system one supports (democracy versus the "dictatorship of the proletariat").[10] Like a ship about to begin a long voyage, a navigational mistake at the outset can lead a crew badly astray, shipwrecked and aground. To use another metaphor, this time from the world of medicine: A physician cannot treat an illness before he diagnoses it correctly; making the wrong diagnosis can make things far worse than they might otherwise be.

Those who champion capitalism embrace a truth we see played out in almost every life on almost any given day: If you link reward to effort, you will get more effort. If you create incentives for a particular kind of behavior, you will see more of that behavior. The book of Thessalonians boils things down to fairly simple terms: "If any would not work, neither should he eat."[11]

A free market can also better our moral condition—not dramatically and not always, but often enough. It places a premium on thrift, savings, and investment. And capitalism, when functioning properly, penalizes certain kinds of behavior—bribery, corruption, and lawlessness among them—because citizens in a free-market society have a huge stake in discouraging such behavior, which is a poison-tipped dagger aimed straight at the heart of prosperity.

In addition, capitalism can act as a civilizing agent. The social critic Irving Kristol argued, correctly, in our view, that the early architects of democratic capitalism believed commercial transactions "would themselves constantly refine and enlarge the individual's sense of his own self-interest, so that in the end the kind of commercial society that was envisaged would be a relatively decent community."[12]

But capitalism, like American democracy itself, is hardly perfect or sufficient by itself. It has a troubling history as well as a glorious one. And like America, it is an ongoing, never-ending experiment, neither self-sustaining nor self-executing. Capitalism requires strong, vital, non-economic and non-political institutions—including the family, churches and other places of worship, civic associations, and schools—to complement it. Such institutions are necessary to allow capitalism to advance human progress.

A capitalist society needs to produce an educated citizenry. It needs to be buttressed by people who possess and who teach others virtues, such as sympathy, altruism, compassion, self-discipline, perseverance, and honesty. And it needs a polity that will abide by laws, contracts, and election results (regardless of their outcome). Without these virtues, capitalism can be eaten from within by venality and used for pernicious ends.

We need to understand that capitalism, like democracy, is part of an intricate social web. Capitalism both depends on it and contributes mightily to it. Morality and capitalism, like morality and democracy, are intimately connected and mutually complementary.[13] They reinforce one another; they need one another; and they are terribly diminished without one another. They are links in a golden chain.

CHAPTER II.
THE ECONOMIC ACHIEVEMENTS OF CAPITALISM

If, in the middle part of the eighteenth century, you were born in London—then, as now, one of the most advanced and modern cities in the world—your chances of living past five years of age would be estimated to be as low as 25 percent.[14]

If you were fortunate enough to make it past five years old, the life that awaited you would not be encouraging. Londoners lived in a world in which "violence, disorder and brutal punishment…were still part of the normal background of life."[15] So were hunger and disease. In London and Paris, "almost every ten years, plague, disease or famine would kill as many as 10,000 people in a couple of weeks"[16]—at a time when the entire population of both countries was less than 40 million.

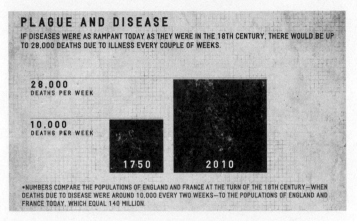

PLAGUE AND DISEASE

IF DISEASES WERE AS RAMPANT TODAY AS THEY WERE IN THE 18TH CENTURY, THERE WOULD BE UP TO 28,000 DEATHS DUE TO ILLNESS EVERY COUPLE OF WEEKS.

28,000 DEATHS PER WEEK

10,000 DEATHS PER WEEK

1750   2010

•NUMBERS COMPARE THE POPULATIONS OF ENGLAND AND FRANCE AT THE TURN OF THE 18TH CENTURY—WHEN DEATHS DUE TO DISEASE WERE AROUND 10,000 EVERY TWO WEEKS—TO THE POPULATIONS OF ENGLAND AND FRANCE TODAY, WHICH EQUAL 140 MILLION.

As you walked the streets, it would not be unusual for you to see children abandoned and left to die. You would as likely as not find yourself in or on the verge of pauperism. You would probably be illiterate. And the odds are high that you would be part of the mass of unskilled or poorly skilled workers—perhaps an agricultural worker or a hand-loom weaver. If so, most of your income would be used to pay for the bare necessities of life.[17]

If you were lucky enough to have a job, it would be almost certainly seasonal, insecure, and subject to sudden interruptions. For many people, this created problems of debt, for which the punishment was imprisonment. "Drinking, gambling, and debt were links in a chain of misfortune which it was difficult to escape," according to the British historian M. Dorothy George.[18]

For all but the most talented, opportunities for advancement were limited. Upward mobility was possible for "the versatile, the pushing and the strong" but difficult for the "unenterprising and the weak."[19] Notoriously harsh conditions existed for factory workers—many of them children—and "child labor from about the age of six was naturally an obstacle to education."[20] Leisure was a foreign concept to the working class. And rigid class distinctions also posed challenges for advancement. In George's words, "it was an age of minute social distinctions": "Lines were drawn between the artisan and the labourer, the master and the journeyman, as they were drawn between the ledger and the housekeeper."[21]

In sum: If you were born in London before the dawn of modern capitalism, the norm was destitution and grinding poverty, widespread illiteracy, illness and disease, and early death. And, even worse, your children could expect a similar fate. The possibility for progress was almost nonexistent for your progeny.

THE INDUSTRIAL REVOLUTION AND ITS IMPACT

The dismal living standards in eighteenth-century London were a result, in part, of living in the pre-capitalist economic systems of the time. These systems did not allow for sustained economic growth and all the good (including intergenerational wealth-building) that would spring forth from it.

In a relatively short period of time, though, the engine of capitalism began to change things, in some instances dramatically so. In the words of the sociologist Daniel Bell:

> Modern capitalism began with the Industrial Revolution…with the technological changes of the creation of machinery for the mechanical production of goods, the laying of thousands of miles of track for the railroads, the invention of steamships that could move faster than wind, and the sociological migration—a total change of life—of hundreds of thousands of persons into cities. All these were a transformation of life hitherto unknown in human history.[22]

This period saw the rise of international markets, trading corporations, and the accumulation of capital; a turn toward free markets and free institutions; and the development of a large middle class for the first time in history. It was a "hinge point" in history, when one way of life gave way to another, and out of it eventually arose wealth and innovations that helped improve the lives and well-being of people on a scale that was previously unimaginable. Even Karl Marx and Frederick Engels conceded, in *The Communist Manifesto*, that capitalism "has created more massive and more colossal productive forces than have all preceding generations together."[23]

But along with the blessings of capitalism came a curse—one that was not a product of capitalism but was instead incidental to the transformations it had launched: tremendous social dislocation and trauma. This was on vivid display during the start of the Industrial Revolution, when the factories that sprung up were often inhumane, with children as young as eight working fourteen hours or more per day in mills and mines.[24] Urbanization caused many people to flee farms for cities, which split apart closely-knit communities and a long-standing way of life.

The near-miraculous amelioration of one set of problems, then—problems that had plagued human society since its inception—created another set. Charles Dickens, a gifted novelist and a fierce critic of the poverty and social stratification he witnessed in England, portrayed the harsh effects of the Industrial Revolution in books like *Oliver Twist* and *Hard Times*. William Blake, in his short poem "Jerusalem," an apocryphal story of Jesus traveling to England, wrote about "these dark Satanic Mills"—a reference to the destructive effects of the Industrial Revolution on factories and community life at the Albion Flour Mills, which were close to Blake's home in England. And the first Luddites (named after Ned Ludd, who is believed to have destroyed two large mechanical knitting machines, called "stocking frames," in the English village of Anstey) appeared in Nottingham in the early 1800s. Knitters destroyed machines that made stockings at prices that undercut skilled craftsmen, part of an organized resistance to technological changes that threatened people's livelihoods and their settled ways of life.

These concerns, while real, should be set against the enormous *progress* that resulted from the advent of modern capitalism, whether we are talking about wealth-creation, material comforts, or overall standard of living. In addition, it is only fair to compare life *during* the Industrial Revolution to life *before* the Industrial Revolution, which was, as we have already documented, often bleak, cruel, and short.

THE RISE (AND FALL) OF COMMUNISM

The collateral effects of the Industrial Revolution were significant. They tugged at many human hearts. And they sparked a powerful intellectual counter-reaction, which manifested itself in the rise of communism.

Capitalism is a system in which "all that is holy is profaned," Karl Marx wrote; he believed capitalism turned the laborer into a "fragment of a man, degrade[d] him to the level of appendage of a machine."[25] Marx, who co-authored with Friedrich Engels the *Manifesto of the Communist Party* (more popularly known as *The Communist Manifesto*), argued that communism would be the final stage in society, achieved through a proletarian (or working-class) revolution, and leading to an abundance of goods and services and social prosperity. "The

Communists disdain to conceal their views and aims," is how the manifesto ends. "They openly declare that their ends can be attained only by the forcible overthrow of all existing social conditions. Let the ruling classes tremble at a Communistic revolution. The proletarians have nothing to lose but their chains. They have a world to win. Workers of the world, unite!" In other words, Marx envisioned a world with the benefits of capitalism, but without its costs.

Not surprisingly, this was not possible. Even worse, it turned out that communism—a political and economic theory that abolishes private ownership and embraces collectivism and (in theory) a classless society—shackled more people in more chains than any other political theory in history. Communism fundamentally misread human nature and, in fact, sowed the seeds of its own destruction. It was communism, not capitalism, which led to the ruination of societies, the weakening of vital social institutions, rampant corruption, and repression.

Part of the reason for communism's failure is that the over-whelming concentration of power into the hands of a few leads to abuse and corruption like night follows day. "Power tends to corrupt, and absolute power corrupts absolutely," is how the historian and moralist John Emerich Edward Dalberg Acton, better known as Lord Acton, put it.

But communism's problem is not just its concentration of power into the hands of a few people; all other manners of tyrannies and autocracies also do that. Rather, communism's particularly fiendish depredations rise from some additional malignancies that are unique to it, including a philosophy of history (the historical dialectic) that both enshrines atheism and essentially deifies the state and its leaders. This provides an ends-justifies-the-means rationalization for any and all violence conducted by the state, all in the service of ushering in a utopian, classless society.

There is also within communism a presumption of the state's omnicompetence over all human behavior; because communism grants the state control over economic behavior, it is an easy and almost inevitable logical leap for the state to then control all other human behavior, including the political and religious realms.

Finally, the materialistic mindset of communism essentially treats human beings as merely economic units in the service of the state. Because of this materialism and the denial of the transcendent properties of the human spirit, the individual has little or no worth except for use by the state.

All of this explains why there is not a single example in history of a communist government that was not dictatorial and did not tyrannize its citizens.

The manifestations of this form of collectivism—the principle of control by the state of all means of productive and economic

activity—is a catalogue of immense and even incomprehensible human horror, from the estimated 65 million deaths under Mao in China; to the more than 20 million Russians who perished under Stalin and Lenin; to the almost 2 million Cambodians—comprising around one quarter of the entire population—who died under the Pol Pot regime.[26]

This last record is worth pausing over. During his time in power, Pol Pot, the leader of Cambodia, forced urban dwellers to relocate to the countryside to work on collective farms and forced-labor projects. The goal, according to this revolutionary communist leader, was to "restart civilization" in "Year Zero." His goal was "building socialism without a model"[27]—a society that was classless, without money, without books, without hospitals, and without religion. What the Cambodians got instead was forced labor, slavery, starvation, mass executions, and wholesale slaughter. Even the worst predations of capitalism count as child's play compared to these acts of systematic genocide.

WHY CAPITALISM TRIUMPHS OVER COMMUNISM

Capitalism, unlike communism, has adjusted to the human difficulties it has generated. It has improved over time. Rather than destroy the greatest wealth-producing engine in history, far-sighted capitalists decided to develop necessary reforms; to sand off capitalism's rougher edges; and to use some of the surplus generated by capitalism to help cushion those on the receiving end of its blows. These early capitalists accepted the fact that government would play a role in the system because they knew that capitalism, despite its many merits, had inherent limitations. It was capable of failures. And so, government would sometimes be called upon to step into the breach, to set rules and to keep order, and, in some instances, to act as an emollient.

This meant, in a practical sense, building a social safety net in the form of health, accident, disability, old-age, and unemployment insurance. It meant that the state began to regulate the conditions of factory work. And it meant that government was responsible for breaking up the concentrated power of trusts and monopolies.

These and other regulatory measures were championed by progressives like German's Otto von Bismarck and England's

Benjamin Disraeli in the nineteenth century and Teddy Roosevelt and Winston Churchill in the twentieth century. These reformers understood that in order for capitalism to endure—in order to make it morally defensible and to prevent the spread of communism throughout the European continent and beyond—capitalism could not be indifferent to pressing human needs. It must have the capacity to assist people through wrenching economic and social transitions. It had to reform in order to flourish; and, for the most part, capitalism has done just that.

The results have been staggering. In places where capitalism has taken root and flowered, income and living standards have shot up. Adam Smith's "universal opulence,"[28] though an impossible goal, sometimes seems almost within reach.

In these developed, first-world, capitalist nations, extreme economic poverty has been largely eliminated. There is an abundance of food. Literacy is commonplace; so are clean water, vaccinations, and access to advanced medical care. Scientific and technological breakthroughs have helped people to live far longer and far better lives. Take, for example, the enormous strides in medicine and genetic research. Prosperous societies can afford these good things.

Of course, capitalism cannot claim all the credit for these advancements, but it *does* deserve of a good deal of the credit.

Why? Because the advancements we are talking about are the fruits of economic growth and material wealth.

In contrast, in areas of the world that have been fenced off from capitalism—places like Sub-Saharan Africa and the Arab Middle East—people live under brutal tyrannies, political corruption, malnutrition, and even starvation; social and technological progress is stymied, economies are stagnant, and the quality of life is dismal.

For example, in 2008, the infant mortality rate in the United States was 6.6 per 1,000 live births. In Sierra Leone, the rate was 158 per 1,000 live births. Of the twenty countries with the highest infant mortality rates in 2008, eighteen were in Africa.[29] In 2009, life expectancy in the United States was estimated to be seventy-eight years. In Swaziland, life expectancy was about thirty-two years. Of the thirty-four countries with the lowest life expectancy, thirty-three are in Africa.[30]

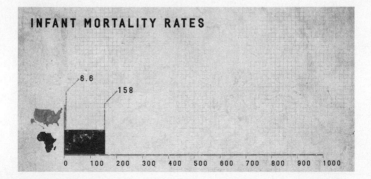

In the words of American University Professor of Economics George Ayittey:

> Africa's salvation doesn't lie in begging and begging for more aid, and as an African, I find it very, very humiliating. We're talking about a continent which is tremendously rich in mineral resources. You name the mineral—gold, diamonds, titanium—you find all that in Africa and our leaders have mismanaged the resources. Look, the salvation of Africa lies in Africa going back to its roots and building upon its own indigenous institutions. There were markets in Africa. There was free trade in Africa. If you go to our villages, you'll find participatory democracy there. *The problem that happened after independence was that our leaders rejected the market system as a Western institution and tried to destroy it and they also rejected democracy. This is why the continent started its road to ruination.*[31]

Take as another example the differences between East and West Germany before the fall of the Berlin Wall, or the differences between North and South Korea today. In both cases, the countries are linguistically and ethnically the same—yet the differences in infant mortality and life-span, in wealth and consumption, and in happiness itself are dramatic.[32]

It is also true that wealthy, capitalist countries are far better equipped to absorb natural calamities than are poor ones.

Consider the earthquake that resulted in mass death and misery on the impoverished island of Haiti in January 2010. As the *Wall Street Journal* put it:

> The earthquake is…a reminder that while natural calamities do not discriminate between rich countries and poor ones, their effects almost invariably do. The 1994 Northridge quake was nearly as powerful as the one that struck Haiti, but its human toll was comparatively slight. The difference is a function of a wealth-generating and law-abiding society that can afford, among other things, the expense of proper building codes.
>
> In the long term, the best defense against future natural disasters is to promote the political and economic conditions that can move people out of the slums and shanties that easily become death traps.[33]

Societies without free markets, then, are—by virtually every meaningful measure—far worse off. The differences between capitalism and its alternatives could not be any sharper, the verdict any more obvious. Capitalism has done more to lift people out of abject poverty than any other system in human history. All the other models—including collectivism, socialism, and communism—have proved to be deeply flawed, and their human effects are often calamitous. Every tree is known by its fruit, Jesus said; and every economic system must be judged by its real-world effects.

Readers may assume that collectivist systems are in the ash-heap of history, that the wolf of socialism is no longer at the door. But this would be a mistake. Leaders like Venezuela's Hugo Chavez promise to take their people down the same hole as did the socialist leaders of the twentieth century. In a 2007 speech, Mr. Chavez, echoing the words of past socialist figures, said: "Those who want to go directly to hell, they can follow capitalism… And those of us who want to build heaven here on earth, we will follow socialism."[34] In point of fact, if we are not vigilant, the lessons of free-market progress will fade from memory. If they are forgotten, there will be enormous economic and human ramifications, all for the worse.

The twentieth-century economist Friedrich Hayek's insight about the use of markets versus state planning has been thoroughly vindicated: No group of people, regardless of how smart, wise, or imaginative they believe themselves to be, can know enough to oversee the centralized planning of a system that will enable human flourishing. Our lives are simply too complex, our daily decisions too many, our capacity to predict the future too limited, for centralized control to be feasible. The best people in all the world cannot coordinate entire social and economic systems, and the best people in all the world are very rarely in power.

CHAPTER III.
CAPITALISM, ETHICS, AND RELIGIOUS FAITH

All of this would be well and good, some say, if the case for capitalism were only economic and not moral. Capitalism may ameliorate poverty; it may lift people out of mass misery; and it may even produce hitherto undreamt-of material wealth. But it also creates spiritual impoverishment. It enervates human character. The very characteristics that gave rise to capitalism in the first place—prudence, self-restraint, patience, and the ability to delay gratification, and what is sometimes called the "Protestant work ethic"—are eventually undermined by the success of capitalism. After all, capitalism rewards greed— does it not? Daniel Bell called this the "cultural contradictions of capitalism."[35]

Because of this concern about the morality, rather than the efficiency, of the market system, the John Templeton Foundation in Autumn 2008 asked some distinguished individuals to answer the question, "Does the free market corrode moral character?"[36]

Several of the participants answered in the affirmative, arguing that capitalism stoked venality, acquisitiveness, and unhealthy competition among people. Some argued that capitalism undermines community and family bonds because it places a premium on mobility and increases separation of work from family life. And still others said that the profit motive drives people to produce crude and exploitive forms of entertainment, whether in music, on television, or via the Internet.

HOW CAPITALISM FOSTERS MORALITY

In responding to these charges against capitalism—some of which we are in sympathy with—we begin with an obvious counterpoint: The material progress that flows from capitalism is no small matter. Lifting people out of poverty is a hugely impressive and important moral achievement. Easing the pain of life is commendable. So is delivering goods to the great mass of the people—something that capitalism, alone among economic systems, has achieved.

To put it another way: No economic system in history has come nearly as close as capitalism to lifting the needy out of their affliction, to raising the poor from the dust.

There is a certain irony in the fact that capitalism is best at doing what it is most often accused of doing worst: distributing wealth to people at every social stratum rather than simply to elites. The evidence of history is clear on this point—the poor gain the most from capitalism,[37] in part because, in most other economic systems, the game is rigged for the well-to-do. "The capitalist engine is first and last an engine of mass production," is how the eco-

nomist Joseph Schumpeter put it, "which unavoidably means also production for the masses…. It is the cheap cloth, the cheap fabric, boots, motor cars and so on that are the typical achievements of capitalist production and not as a rule improvements that would mean much to the rich man."[38]

Schumpeter was an economist and political scientist, not a theologian. But his point finds some grounding in Christian and Jewish Scripture. In Deuteronomy, we are told that the God of the Hebrew Bible, Yahweh, "executes for the fatherless and the widow, and loves the sojourner, giving him food and clothing."[39]

In the New Testament, when speaking about what individuals owed to "the least of these," Jesus said: "For I was hungry and you gave me food, I was thirsty and you gave me drink."[40]

We are not making the preposterous claim that God favors capitalism; we simply believe that many Biblical ends are advanced through capitalism far better than through any of its alternatives.

Next, there is the matter of coercion. Totalitarian countries aim to exercise almost complete control over their subjects, to regulate virtually every area of life (political, social, and economic). They are soul-destroying regimes. The great playwright and former Czech president Vaclav Havel, in writing about daily life under communist rule in Eastern Europe, described the regime as permeated with lies and hypocrisy, requiring its subjects, even if they did not believe in this "ideological pseudo-reality," to "live within the lie."[41] This is just one part of the dehumanizing and demoralizing effects of state planning and control.

Capitalism, like democracy, requires private spheres of human action that are beyond the reach of a "nanny state." It *allows* people the freedom to act, which is an essential part of human dignity—and it *trusts* people to act, which is consistent with the belief held by many people of faith that humans are made in God's image.

Capitalism also fosters certain habits, encouraging individuals to make free and informed choices on most of the matters they confront in their daily lives. It is no coincidence, then, that there has never been a free society that has been hostile to free enterprise. The requirements of one are the requirements of the other; the market system and political democracy go hand-in-hand.

The People's Republic of China is trying to prove that it can combine economic liberalization with a police state; we will see how the experiment ends up. Many believe that capitalism will ultimately loosen that state's iron grip. Representative government is the most humane political system ever created, the only one that respects basic human rights. And since free markets are central to free societies, they are also responsible for advancing human rights. This achievement is not lauded nearly often enough.

Neither, we would add, is this one: Capitalism is not only a friend of economic and political liberty; it is a friend of what many people believe to be the first of all freedoms: religious liberty.

Religious liberty lays down what is, for people of the Christian faith, one of the most important preconditions of all: that people can worship God *freely* and without coercion. Because of capitalism's intrinsic limits on the authority of the state, there is an undeniable link between free markets and freedom of religion, of conscience, and of expression. It is no coincidence that religion is outlawed in societies where the state is all-powerful, where the state becomes a stand-in for God.

Capitalism also tends to moderate warlike tendencies in people, turning their attention from armed conflict to commerce. The motto of Amsterdam is *Commercium et Pas* ("Commerce Fosters Peace.")[42] This is not to suggest that capitalist societies don't go to war; they do. The United States itself was involved in several wars during the twentieth century, including two World Wars. But those wars pitted free societies against repressive and aggressive ones. What one does not observe is politically and economically free societies taking up arms against one another.

If capitalism were more widespread, we believe it is safe to say that world peace would be also.

Capitalism connects people of different nations and cultures in unprecedented ways through commercial activities and interactions. The English philosopher and political theorist John Stuart Mill wrote about this in the middle of the nineteenth century:

> The economical advantages of commerce are surpassed in importance by those of its effects, which are intellectual and moral. It is hardly possible to overrate the value, in the present low state of human improvement, of placing human beings in contact with persons dissimilar to themselves, and with modes of thought and action unlike those with which they are familiar… There is no nation which does not need to borrow from others, not merely particular arts or practices, but essential points of character in which its own type is inferior…. It may be said without exaggeration that the great extent and rapid increase in international trade, in being the principal guarantee of the peace of the world, is the great permanent security for the uninterrupted progress of the ideas, the institutions, and the character of the human race.[43]

Jagdish Bhagwati, University Professor of Economics and Law at Columbia University, provides an example: When in the 1980s Japanese male executives brought their wives with them to Western cities like New York, Paris, and London, these traditional wives embraced concepts like women's rights and equality. "When they retuned to Japan," he writes, "they became agents of social reform."[44]

Capitalism's chief western alternative today is social democracy. Among the greatest dangers of social democracy is that the state creates dependency among the citizenry. This, in turn, creates passivity and indolence, the mitigation of individual initiative and the draining of entrepreneurial energy. A culture of dependency is antithetical to the spirit of democratic capitalism. Under social democracy, the individual is less autonomous; under capitalism, she is more autonomous.

Capitalism, then, tends to foster self-sufficiency and self-reliance—in work, a sense of vocation, meaning and fulfillment; and in human affairs, civility, good manners, and reliability (these are, after all, traits important to people who are buying and selling among one another). As the philosopher and theologian Michael Novak points out: "One of the main functions of a capitalist economy [is] to defeat envy...the most destructive of social evils."[45] And unlike what came before it—including feudal societies and hereditary monarchies—capitalism rewards people based on ability rather than birth status, on individual merit rather than blood lines.

PROTECTING CAPITALISM FROM CORRUPTION

Having said all this, in response to the question posed by the Templeton Foundation—"Does the free market corrode moral character?"—the answer is: It can. Capitalism, for all its benefits and for all the good it has done, is not flawless. And under certain conditions it can become exploitive and self-destructive. Warnings about such evils can be found in the Hebrew Bible and the New Testament, condemning those who manipulate the economy for their own selfish purposes (Proverbs 3:27–28; 11:26 and James 5:1–6); who take advantage of the poor (Leviticus 19:13, Amos 5:11–12; 8:5–6); and who are consumed by greed and avarice.[46]

In recent years, we have seen this corruption take many forms, including the investment banker Ivan Boesky's insider-trading scandals in the 1980s; former WorldCom chairman Bernard Ebbers' orchestration of a multibillion-dollar accounting fraud operation in 2002; Enron officials' illegal inflation of profits, concealment of a billion dollars in debt, and manipulation of the energy market; and former NASDAQ stock exchange chairman Bernard Madoff's operation of a Ponzi scheme that defrauded thousands of investors of billions of dollars. These are high-profile cases; there are an uncounted number of examples of corruption that could be added to the list. Where human beings are found, so is corruption, whether a country is capitalist or socialist.

Upon reflection, however, these are not cases of free markets corroding moral character. They are cases of poor moral character corroding free markets. The answer is not less capitalism. It is better capitalists.

No economic system can be expected to teach morality; this is simply beyond its scope. Many human needs and desires—love of country, love for another person, devotion to God; the joy inspired by beautiful music, art, and athletic competition; the excitement of reading a great book or being in the company of great friends—are simply beyond the reach of capitalism. Capitalism can provide people with comfortable lives, but not truly meaningful ones. "Capitalist efficiency may…be regarded as the most useful precondition for a good life in a good society," Irving Kristol once wrote. "But one has to go beyond Adam Smith, or capitalism itself, to discover the other elements that are wanted."[47]

"A man's life does not consist in the abundance of his possession," is how Jesus put it in the Gospel of Luke.[48]

A free economy, like a democratic political community, requires certain preconditions in order to best function, most especially a strong civic and social order and a shared belief in an underlying moral code. If people are not acting as good citizens or upholding basic ethical standards—if they routinely lie and cheat; if their word is not their bond; if they feel no attachment or obligation to others; if they have not been instructed on "their rights, interests, and duties, as men and citizens"[49]—then no political or economic system based on individual liberty can long survive.

So where should moral instruction come from? Not primarily from government. In some instances, government can have an ennobling function, and by its actions it can shape moral sentiments.[50] But government is a terribly blunt instrument. It sees things in black-and-white terms, with people's behavior falling into one of two camps: illegal or legal (and therefore permissible). The limitation of this, of course, is that some things are legal but wrong (marital infidelity, for example), and some things are permissible but harmful (such as obesity). Much of life is lived in areas shaded with gray.

Government cannot easily or effectively inculcate virtue in individuals—and even if it could, it would be ceding far too much power to the state to grant it the authority to mold human character. That responsibility belongs predominantly to what authors Peter Berger and Richard John Neuhaus call "mediating institutions"[51]—neighborhoods, churches and other houses of worship, voluntary associations, community organizations, local schools, and especially the family—that intervene between individual citizens and government.

These institutions teach children right from wrong, what to cherish and value, what habits to develop, and what aspirations to aim for. We learn these things through instruction and example; by what we read, see and hear; and by the company we keep and the role models we set before us. "What we have loved others will love, and we will teach them how," is how the poet William Wordsworth put it.[52]

The moral education of the young—teaching them self-discipline and compassion, responsibility and loyalty, honesty and perseverance—is the responsibility of parents and adults of every generation. No task on earth is more personally fulfilling—and none plays a more vital role in creating a decent society and a flourishing civilization.

The morality of capitalism depends on the cultural soil and social climate from which it emerges. If it exists in an amoral or an immoral culture—where rules don't apply and "anything goes," where people are urged to give up on the "inhibitions of civilization" and follow "the rebellious imperative of self"[53]—capitalism will become a destructive force. If, on the other hand, capitalism exists in a morally anchored society, it can promote important virtues.

To put the matter directly, those who care about fostering a vibrant moral and cultural order and those who care about promoting free markets depend on one another. If their agendas are pried apart, both will eventually be undone. If they are twinned together, both will flourish.

Whatever cultural complications capitalism might create, these can—with the active support of character-shaping institutions—be overcome. The history of the last three centuries is indisputable: The rewards and benefits of capitalism far outweigh the drawbacks. In our view, it is not really a close call.

CHAPTER IV.
IS CAPITALISM UNJUST?

Opponents and critics of capitalism often base their critiques on two connected claims: first, that capitalism generates and exacerbates inequality; second, that equality itself should be the highest social good.

In America in the 1970s, several influential academic voices broke with previous political philosophers from the ancient Greeks to the American founding fathers in arguing that the fundamental task of the state is to end inequality. They believed that bringing about equality is a requirement of a just social order. The legal philosopher Ronald Dworkin went so far as to say that "a more equal society is a better society even if its citizens prefer inequality."[54] Those views, which were unusual at the time, are now more common, not simply in the academy but also within wider society.

The core of this belief is that inequality is intrinsically bad and even intolerable. According to the new egalitarians, America is a rich country—but it is also a shamefully unequal one.

Radical disparities in wealth are not only unfair; they undermine social cohesion and fuel envy, resentment, and unhappiness. To these critics, capitalism, the economic engine of democracy, is responsible for promoting inequality in income, in standards of living, and in social status.

Whatever good capitalism may do, this argument goes, inequality is a large black mark against it.

In order to correct these social ills, these critics say, government must narrow the income gap between the haves and the have-nots. The remedy most often advocated is the redistribution of income, a task to be undertaken by the state. "Unbridled capitalism" needs to be reigned in—and the state should reign it in by reallocating resources in a more humane and just manner.

UNDERSTANDING INEQUALITY

There is a lot to untangle in this egalitarian worldview. Perhaps the best way to start is by questioning the two propositions directly: Is income inequality inherently unjust? If so, is it the duty of government to "level the playing field" in order to achieve greater equality? The answer to both questions, we believe, is no, for reasons rooted in moral philosophy and human experience.

First, we note that jettisoning capitalism will not lead to greater equality. That claim, repeated like an incantation, does not correspond to the lessons of history. Even societies that have committed themselves to the goal of equality have not been able to achieve it. As the sociologist and theologian Peter Berger, author of *The Capitalist Revolution*, has written:

> We continue to hear that, yes indeed, capitalism increases prosperity, but at the price of gross inequalities....[N]othing has changed my mind about the strong probability that the notion of a trade-off between growth and equality is false. The weight of the evidence indicates that the Kuznets effect does indeed hold [increased inequality as a modern economy takes off, with a leveling-off occurring within a reasonable time thereafter], but that it holds regardless of whether economic growth takes place under a capitalist or a socialist system. In other words, the basic choice between capitalism and socialism is irrelevant to the issue of equality, except that capitalism greatly accelerates the growth process, thus accelerating both the inegalitarian and the egalitarian phases of the Kuznets curve.
>
> It follows that to opt for capitalism is not to opt for inequality at the price of growth; rather, it is to opt for an accelerating transformation of society. This undoubtedly produces tensions and exacts costs, but one must ask whether these are likely to be greater than

the tensions and costs engendered by socialist stagnation. Moreover, the clearer view of the European socialist societies that has now become public radically debunks the notion that, whatever else may have ailed these societies, they were more egalitarian than those in the West: they were nothing of the sort.... The claims to greater equality are even hollower in the much poorer socialist societies in the Third World (China emphatically included).[55]

We have seen time and again that centrally planned systems not only fail to equalize human society, they also have "corroded character far more damagingly and with fewer benefits in terms of efficiency and productivity."[56] In the Soviet Union, for example, corruption was "ubiquitous" and "people with the most highly developed survival skills and the fewest moral scruples did best."[57]

Corruption obviously isn't *unique* to communist regimes, but it is endemic to them. The reason is that the strongest antidotes to corruption are transparency (freedom of the press, an open political system, open and trust-based capital markets); accountability (institutional checks and balances, free and fair elections); and a culture of integrity (internal restraints practiced by citizens and communities, an expectation of honest behavior, etc).

Communist regimes either resist or erode all three of these pillars. Government is inevitably dominated by a secretive politburo and/or autocrats who permit no independent scrutiny or press freedom, while state control of the economy eliminates transparent, trust-based capital markets (which depend on honest reporting of profits and losses to facilitate the voluntary exchange of goods and services). Dictatorships, by their nature, resist all accountability. And communism seeks to erode civil society and culture and the mediating institutions which enable self-government, replacing it all with the state. Human nature being what it is, when there are no restraints against it, corruption will almost inevitably develop.

Corruption is also often the only recourse of citizens when their formal economy or government does not function efficiently (hence the rise of the black markets in North Korea, Cuba, and elsewhere). Since communist regimes almost invariably don't work well, citizens often resort to corrupt practices (bribes, smuggling, etc) as their only option to get through daily life within the dysfunctional system.

Even the Israeli *kibbutzim* (communal farms or settlements), which are committed to a radical egalitarian ideal and based on the Marxist axiom "from each according to his abilities to each according to his needs," have failed, even though these communities were voluntary and drew from a small, self-selected, homogeneous, and highly committed pool of people—that is, one that was most likely to succeed. Rather than contentment and harmony within these communities, there was resentment toward those who were not carrying their weight but benefited anyway, making the *kibbutz* a place where "small differences were magnified, and became festering sores."[58]

"Nowhere is the failure of socialism clearer than in the radical transformation of the Israeli *kibbutz*," the Nobel Prize–winning economist Gary Becker has written.[59] Becker, who visited a *kibbutz* several decades ago, observed firsthand the disharmony created among *kibbutz* residents by even the slightest advancement of one of its members. During the 1980s, *kibbutzim* faced near financial ruin and many of them either evolved into private enterprises or declared bankruptcy. Since then, the majority of *kibbutzim* have become populated by families living in privately-owned homes; workers are now compensated according to their level of productivity.

As Becker describes, the excitement of living in the collective environment quickly faded within a generation:

> They did not realize that while the zeal of pioneers, and the result of revolutions, could sustain a collectivist and other-serving mentality for a short while, these could not be maintained as the pioneers died off or became disillusioned, and as circumstances became less revolutionary.[60]

A thirty-year *kibbutz* resident echoed Becker's finding, saying:

> People wanted more control over their own lives and
> economics. They wanted to make their own decisions,
> and have their own car and their own telephone. It is
> very difficult to live this strong communal life. It is
> very tiring.[61]

Next, we ask what people have in mind when they object to
income inequality. What would proper redistribution of income
look like? Should everyone have the same income, regardless
of one's occupation and station in life? Should LeBron James
make as much as a hotdog vender? If not, who should decide
just how much a mega-athlete and movie star, a singer and
comedian, an author and book editor, a *New York Times* reporter
and the president of Microsoft ought to make? Should their
income be set by the federal government? If not, should income
equality be achieved by taxing at such a prohibitive rate that the
gap between LeBron James and the hotdog vender is largely
eliminated? And, if so, what would be the negative impact on
the performance and output of people who now earn huge sala-
ries? In short, what lengths are the new egalitarians willing to
go in order to eliminate or reduce the gap? And at what cost?

Two clarifications are in order here. The first is to recognize
that some forms of income inequality have nothing at all to do
with individual talent or skill but rather the luck of the draw.
One person might inherit great wealth from his parents, based

on nothing he has done; another person might be born into circumstances that make her obstacles to success vastly more difficult than others. In fact, philanthropy is often motivated by an admirable impulse to help people facing unfair circumstances. Few people are inclined to defend inequality for its own sake; the concern is that the remedy most often employed to reduce inequality—increasing the power, size, and reach of the federal government as it takes on the role as society's great equalizer—can have baleful consequences while still failing to eliminate inequality.

It also needs to be said that sometimes inequality does not follow merit. And when that occurs, the question then becomes: Should a society, when it is above subsistence and when merit is not involved, take away resources from the rich so they will have less? To do so is not redistribution to alleviate suffering; it is redistribution to satisfy envy.

The second clarification is to acknowledge that a progressive tax system—one that levies a proportionately higher tax rate on those with higher incomes in order to increase revenues and offset income inequalities—exists in the United States and, within reason, is unobjectionable to most people. Adam Smith explained why when he wrote:

> The necessaries of life occasion the great expense of the poor. They find it difficult to get food, and the greater part of their little revenue is spent in getting it.

The luxuries and vanities of life occasion the principal expense of the rich, and a magnificent house embellishes and sets off to the best advantage all the other luxuries and vanities which they possess. A tax upon house-rents, therefore, would in general fall heaviest upon the rich; and in this sort of inequality there would not, perhaps, be anything very unreasonable. It is not very unreasonable that the rich should contribute to the public expense, not only in proportion to their revenue, but something more than in that proportion.[62]

What Adam Smith is commending here, of course, is not equality of outcome; instead, it is more in line with the Biblical admonition that to whom much is given much is required. A progressive tax system is a world apart from the belief that using the federal government to redress income inequality is the *sine qua non* of a just and legitimate social order. Efforts to achieve level income have failed everywhere they have occurred because such efforts cut against the human grain. Yet even if it *were* achievable, we would *still* reject it on moral and philosophical grounds.

ECONOMIC JUSTICE AND RELIGIOUS TEACHING

Here, we want to take up directly the argument that Biblical justice can be understood as "social justice" and "economic justice"—terms which are used to justify fierce attacks on capitalism, the creation of wealth, and the profit motive. Some argue that income redistribution, with the aim of income equality, is a biblical principle; and that solidarity with the poor means leveling differences in income, taking from the powerful in order to aid the poor and the oppressed.

We dissent from this view. First, we simply reject the notion that God demands a particular economic system. Second, as we have already demonstrated, if empowering and improving the condition of the poor is the goal—if, as Jim Wallis of *Sojourners* magazine said, "the gospel is biased in favor of the poor and oppressed"[63]—then capitalism is the economic system that makes that most possible. You cannot will the ends without willing the means—and in this context, free market economies are the means.

The God of the Hebrew Bible and New Testament hates oppression and injustice. He warns against those who withhold wages or take unfair advantage of those in debt. He commends charity. And Saint Paul warns that love of money is the root of all kinds of evil. Yet private property—which is neither explicitly condemned nor defended in Scripture—is taken for granted. The commandment "Thou shalt not steal" presupposed the right to private property.

"Why does Scripture require restitution, including multiple restitution, in cases of theft, even if paying the restitution requires selling oneself into slavery?" Professor E. Calvin Beisner has asked.[64] We read in Acts that Barnabas, a godly man, "sold a field that belonged to him, then brought the money, and laid it at the apostles' feet."[65] In addition, many great men of God were wealthy (including Abraham and Solomon). As for using the redistribution of income to achieve egalitarianism: If it is done at all, it is done voluntarily, as an act of charity, out of gratitude for what God has done, *not* as an action of the state, through coercion.[66]

To underscore why forced egalitarianism is itself unjust, it's worth considering what a professor we know does every semester with his students. He tells them that he will redistribute points on the first exam in order to achieve an equal outcome of results. He then tells his students to imagine that he has taken points off their exam in order to achieve that result. To a person, these students are adamant that such a thing is simply unfair; they have earned their grade, they insist. To take points off their exam in order to give them to someone who scored lower is unfair. That is, of course, precisely the point. The students understood, in very personal terms, that justice is a matter of receiving one's due.

Redistribution has many other problems. First, to distribute income equally among everyone, including those who are idle and lazy, would encourage slothfulness and devalue work.[67] "Lazy hands make a man poor," the book of Proverbs tells us, "but diligent hands bring wealth."[68]

Second, ceding authority to government to equalize income would grant the state a frightening level of power. If one believes in limited government, one cannot insist that the state take on as one of its chief functions the role of leveling differences among citizens and fine-tuning outcomes. As Michael Novak has said, in a free society the state should be *subsidium*.[69] It loses legitimacy as it encroaches into areas where it does not belong.

Third, inequality is often the product of differences in human beings, including differences in intelligence and skills, in drive and determination, in attitude and character. Outcomes are different because *people* are different. That is something we not only need to accept; it is something we should celebrate. It means that people will excel in different fields. And it keeps us from becoming a monochrome society by adding diversity and texture to our lives. As long as people are different we will experience—absent extraordinary coercion—inequality of one sort or another.[70]

"A certain degree of inequality has to be allowed in society if such a society is to preserve human dignity and freedom and to achieve basic standards of justice," Brian Griffiths, a noted international economist and a former top aide to Margaret Thatcher, has put it. Griffiths wrote:

> It is important that people should receive the rewards of their work. But at the same time money involves responsibility and the Christian as steward is called

to share his resources with others. From this perspective libertarianism is one-sided; it emphasizes rights to property to the exclusion of any responsibilities with property: but egalitarianism is also one-sided in that it emphasizes responsibilities to the exclusion of rights. The Christian has a perspective which is unique in that it emphasizes both rights and responsibilities.[71]

Free markets also encourage the kind of creativity that allows individuals to flourish. Pope John Paul II linked the concept of creativity to enterprise and initiative; he called "personal economic enterprise" a fundamental human right.[72] And in his papal encyclical *Sollicitudo Rei Socialis*, he wrote:

Experience shows us that the denial of this right, or its limitation in the name of an alleged "equality" of everyone in society, diminishes, or in practice absolutely destroys, the spirit of initiative, that is to say the creative subjectivity of the citizen. As a consequence, there arises, not so much a true equality as a "leveling down." In the place of creative initiative there appears passivity, dependence and submission to the bureaucratic apparatus which, as the only "ordering" and "decision-making" body—if not also the "owner"—of the entire totality of goods and the means of production, puts everyone in a position of almost absolute dependence....This provokes a sense of frustration or desperation and predisposes people to opt out of national life.[73]

Pope John Paul II believed that embracing liberty as a political concept involved embracing liberty in the economic sphere as well.

Christian teaching, and, in particular, Jesus' Parable of the Talents (found in Matthew 25), offer insight as well. In this parable, a master is about to undertake a journey and gives three servants different amounts of talents (a unit of money at the time) before departing. When he returns from his travels, the master asks each servant to give an account for the money given to them.

The first servant, who had received five talents, "went at once and put his money to work and gained five more." The second servant, who had received two talents, did the same thing and gained two more. Both were praised by the master. The third servant, who had received one talent, buried his talent in the ground for safekeeping. The master called him wicked and lazy, took the talent from him, and gave it to the servant with ten talents.[74]

One interpretation of this parable is that people are meant to work with and improve upon the gifts God has given them. As good stewards, people are expected to be accountable for what they do with the talents they have been given. Talents and skills are not to be hoarded or stashed away or never used in an enterprising manner. Rather, people have an obligation to develop their abilities and resources and use them effectively, intelligently, and to advance good ends.

It's worth adding that the materialist worldview inherent in efforts to eliminate income inequality is at odds with the Christian faith. This worldview assumes that financial relationships define human relationships, that what matters most is our financial standing relative to each other. And of course Christianity, and most other faiths, utterly reject such an outlook.

CONCLUSION

Making income equality a priority of government policy sub-verts equality of opportunity, which is in many ways at the heart of the American Dream. You cannot have both; one necessarily excludes the other.

"The progress by which the poor, honest, industrious and reso-lute man raises himself, that he may work on this own account and hire somebody else...is the great principle for which this government was really formed," Abraham Lincoln said. He went on to say:

> I don't believe in a law to prevent a man from getting rich; it would do more harm than good. So while we do not propose any war upon capital, we do wish to allow the humblest man an equal chance to get rich with everybody else.... I want every man to have the chance—and I believe a black man is entitled to it—in which he *can* better his condition—when he may look forward and hope to be a hired laborer this year and

the next, work for himself afterward, and finally to hire men to work for him! That is the true system.[75]

Lincoln believed upward mobility was the solution to poverty, and this view animated his decisions on everything from the Homestead Act to Morrill Land-Grant College Act.[76]

Allowing individuals the chance to better their condition is a legitimate moral claim that citizens demand of government. Government's goal should be to ensure equality of *opportunity* instead of equality of outcome; to work toward a society where everyone has a fair shot rather than one where government enforces equality. So long as people are provided with, and perceive themselves as having, a legitimate opportunity to succeed, income inequality will not tear at the fabric of a society. Equality of opportunity is, in fact, the best antidote to envy and covetousness. It drains these maladies of their potency and delegitimizes them.

To be committed to equality of opportunity means, in concrete terms, upholding the rule of law, opposing discrimination, promoting first-rate education, and expanding access to capital for those who do not have it and, for unjust reasons, have been denied it.

What fundamentally separates capitalists from those who want to redistribute income is a different concept of justice— "distributive justice" versus what has been called the "productive justice"[77] of capitalism.

For those who that believe economics is a zero-sum game, the only way to mitigate income inequality is through income redistribution. But those who believe in "productive justice" hold to the view that economic growth will create opportunity and wealth for those in every social stratum—and, in the end, generate the best of all worlds: allowing people to succeed without penalizing excellence and achievement and providing opportunity for those at the bottom rungs of the ladder to move up.

It would be silly to contend that income inequality will ever be eliminated, or that failure can be averted, even if everyone gets a fair shot. The causes of income inequality are deep and varied, including family disruption and changing premiums put on certain human skills and human intelligence in a modern society. These factors explain, in part, the social and income stratification we see.

On this subject, it may be best to leave the last word to the French political thinker, historian, and chronicler of America Alexis de Tocqueville, who wrote: "Democracy and socialism have nothing in common but one word, equality. But notice the difference: while democracy seeks equality in liberty, socialism seeks equality in restraint and servitude."[78]

Count us, like most Americans, in the camp of those seeking equality of liberty.

ABOUT THE AUTHORS

Arthur C. Brooks is the president of the American Enterprise Institute for Public Policy Research. Until January 1, 2009, he was the Louis A. Bantle Professor of Business and Government Policy at Syracuse University. He is the author of eight books and many articles on topics ranging from the economics of the arts to applied mathematics. His most recent books include *The Battle: How the Fight Between Free Enterprise and Big Government Will Shape America's Future* (Basic Books, May 2010), *Gross National Happiness* (Basic Books, 2008), *Social Entrepreneurship* (Prentice-Hall, 2008), and *Who Really Cares* (Basic Books, 2006). Before pursuing his work in public policy, Mr. Brooks spent twelve years as a professional French Hornist with the City Orchestra of Barcelona and other ensembles.

Philip Jenkins is the Edwin Erle Sparks Professor of Humanities at Pennsylvania State University, where he has taught since 1980, and a distinguished senior fellow at Baylor University's Institute for Studies of Religion. He is a contributing editor for *The American Conservative,* a columnist for *The Christian Century,* and a regular contributor to *Christianity Today, First Things, Atlantic Monthly, and the New Republic,* among other publications. Mr. Jenkins has written twenty-four books, which have been translated into twelve languages. His recent books include *Jesus Wars: How Four Patriarchs, Three Queens, and Two Emperors Decided What Christians Would Believe for the Next 1,500 Years* (HarperOne, 2010); *The Lost History of Christianity: The*

Thousand-Year Golden Age of the Church in the Middle East, Africa, and Asia—and How It Died (HarperOne, 2008); *and God's Continent: Christianity, Islam, and Europe's Religious Crisis* (Oxford University Press, 2007).

Peter Wehner, former Deputy Assistant to the President and Director of the White House Office of Strategic Initiatives, is a Senior Fellow at the Ethics and Public Policy Center. Mr. Wehner served in the Ronald Reagan and George H. W. Bush administrations prior to becoming deputy director of speech-writing for President George W. Bush in 2001. He writes widely on national security and political, cultural, and religious issues, and is co-author (with Michael J. Gerson) of *City of Man: Religion and Politics in a New Era* (Moody Publishers, 2010).

ENDNOTES

1. Jean-Jacques Rousseau, *The Social Contract and Other Later Political Writings*, edited by Victor Gourevitch (New York: Cambridge University Press, 1997).

2. Thomas Hobbes, *Leviathan*, ch. XIII, XVII (Forgotten Books, 2008), 86 (originally published in 1651).

3. Romans 6:13.

4. Alexander Hamilton, *The Federalist*, no. 15, par. 12, available at http://thomas.loc.gov/home/histdox/fed_15.html.

5. Adam Smith, *The Theory of Moral Sentiments* (Oxford University Press, 1976).

6. Adam Smith, *An Inquiry into the Nature and Causes of the Wealth of Nations*, book X, edited by Edwin Cannan (1904), available at http://www.econlib.org/library/Smith/smWN12.html.

7. Ibid., book IV, ch. II.

8. J. Hector St. John de Crevecoeur, *Letters From an American Farmer*, letter III, par. 8, available at http://xroads.virginia.edu/~hyper/CREV/letter03.html.

9. Smith, *Wealth of Nations*, book I, ch. II.

10. Karl Marx, *The Class Struggles in France, 1848 to 1850* (New York: International Publishers, 1965).

11. 2 Thessalonians 3:10.

12. Irving Kristol, *Neo-Conservatism: The Autobiography of an Idea* (Chicago: Ivan R. Dee, 1999), 282.

13. "As there is a degree of depravity in mankind which requires a certain degree of circumspection and distrust," Madison wrote in *Federalist* No.

55, "so there are other qualities in human nature, which justify a certain portion of esteem and confidence. Republican government presupposes the existence of these qualities in a higher degree than any other form."

14. M. Dorothy George, *London Life in the Eighteenth Century* (Academy Chicago Publishers, 1985), 42. See also Mabel C. Buer, *Health, Wealth and Population in the Early Days of the Industrial Revolution, 1760–1815* (London: George Routledge & Sons, 1926), 30.

15. George, *London Life in the Eighteenth Century*, 4.

16. Michael Novak, *Three in One: Essays on Democratic Capitalism 1976–2000*, edited by Edward W. Younkins (Lanham: Rowman & Littlefield Publishers, 2001), 57.

17. T. S. Ashton, "The Standard of Life of the Workers in England, 1790–1830," in *Capitalism and the Historians*, edited by F. A. Hayek (New York: Routledge, 2003), 159.

18. George, *London Life in the Eighteenth Century,* 311.

19. Buer, *Health, Wealth and Population*, 39.

20. George, *London Life in the Eighteenth Century*, 191.

21. Ibid., 156–57.

22. Daniel Bell, *The Cultural Contradictions of Capitalism* (New York: Basic Books, 1976), 292–93.

23. Karl Marx and Frederick Engels, *The Communist Manifesto*, trans. Samuel Moore (London: Penguin Books, 2002), 225.

24. "Can Capitalism Survive?" *Time*, July 14, 1975, available at http://www.time.com/time/magazine/article/0,9171,917650,00.html (accessed June 18, 2010).

25. Karl Marx, *Capital: A Critique of Political Economy*, vol. I, *The Process of*

Capitalist Production, edited by Frederick Engels and Ernest Untermann, translated by Samuel Moore and Edward Aveling, ch. 25, sec. 4, par. 11 (1906), available at http://www.econlib.org/library/YPDBooks/Marx/mrxCpA. html.

26. Stephane Courtois, Nicolas Werth, Jean-Louis Panne, Andrzej Paczkowski, Karel Bartosek, and Jean-Louis Margolin, *The Black Book of Communism: Crimes, Terror, Repression*, translated by Jonathan Murphy and Mark Kramer (Cambridge: Harvard University Press, 1999).

27. Grant Evans and Kevin Rowley, *Red Brotherhood at War: Indochina since the Fall of Saigon* (London: Verso, 1984).

28. Smith, *Wealth of Nations*, book X.

29. "Secondary School Enrollment, Female, 2000/2004," Population Reference Bureau, available at http://www.prb.org/Datafinder/Topic/Bar. aspx?sort=v&order=d&variable=28.

30. "Life Expectancy at Birth," CIA World Factbook, available at https://www.cia.gov/library/publications/the-world-factbook/rankorder/2102rank. html.

31. Renee Montagne and George Ayittey, "Expert: Africa Needs More than Foreign Aid," National Public Radio, July 6, 2005, available at http://www. npr.org/templates/story/story.php?storyId=4731168 (emphasis added).

32. In 1988, infant mortality in East Germany was 8.1 per 1,000 births, compared with 7.6 per 1,000 births in West Germany. See R. Turner, "Over Past 30 Years, Most Developed Countries Have Had Substantial Declines in Infant Mortality," *Family Planning Perspectives* 23, no. 3 (1991): 139–40. In 1988, life expectancy between birth and age 75 was 66.61 in East Germany compared with 68.04 in West Germany. See World Development Indicators: WDI Online, available at http://publications.worldbank.org/WDI/. Infant mortality in North Korea rose to 19 per 1,000 live births in 2009, compared

with 4.29 for South Korea. See "Background Note: South Korea," Bureau of East Asian and Pacific Affairs, U.S. Department of State, available at http://www.state.gov/r/pa/ei/bgn/2800.htm; "North Koreans' Life Expectancy Falls as Infant Mortality Rises," *Times Online*, available at http://www.timesonline.co.uk/tol/news/world/asia/article7035878.ece (accessed February 22, 2010). Life expectancy at birth in North Korea is 63.81; in South Korea, it is 78.45 years. North Korean GDP per capita (PPP) is $1,800; in South Korea it is $27,700. See "The World Factbook," Central Intelligence Agency, available at https://www.cia.gov/library/publications/the-world-factbook/geos/ks.html. According to the World Values Survey (WVS), East Germany reported an average score of 2.05 on a happiness scale from 0 to 4 (with 4 being the worst); West Germans averaged 1.96. Similarly, on a scale of subjective well-being, East Germany scored 1.62 compared with West Germany's 2.4, with 7.5 being the maximum well-being. See Inglehart, Foa, Peterson, Welzel, "Development, Freedom and Rising Happiness: A Global Perspective 1981–2007," *Perspectives on Psychological Science* 3, no. 4 (2008), available at http://margaux.grandvinum.se/SebTest/wvs/SebTest/wvs/articles/folder_published/article_base_122/files/RisingHappinessPPS.pdf (accessed January 18, 2010). On a scale of 1 to 10 with 10 being the most satisfied, East Germans in 1990 averaged 6.7 while West German respondents averaged 7.2. See World Values Survey 2009, available at http://www.worldvaluessurvey.org/ (accessed Jan. 20, 2009).

33. "Haiti's Tragedy," *Wall Street Journal*, January 14, 2010, available at http://online.wsj.com/article/SB10001424052748703414504575001293421168252.html.

34. "Chavez Launches Biting U.S. Attack," BBC News, March 11, 2007, available at http://news.bbc.co.uk/2/hi/americas/6438753.stm.

35. Bell, *The Cultural Contradictions of Capitalism*.

36. *Does the Free Market Corrode Moral Character? Thirteen Views on the Question*, John

Templeton Foundation, 2008.

37. Michael Novak, "Wealth and Virtue: The Moral Case for Capitalism." *National Review Online*, February 18, 2004, available at http://www.nationalreview.com/novak/novak200402180913.asp (accessed December 29, 2009).

38. Joseph A. Schumpeter, *Capitalism, Socialism, and Democracy*, 3rd Ed. (New York: Harper and Brothers, 1950).

39. Deuteronomy 10:18.

40. Matthew 25:35.

41. Vaclav Havel, *The Power of the Powerless*, edited by John Keane (New York: Palach Press, 1985).

42. See Michael Novak's essay in *Does the Free Market Corrode Moral Character?*, available at http://www.templeton.org/market/PDF/Novak.pdf.

43. John Stuart Mill, *Principles of Political Economy*, book III, ch. XVII, sec. 5 (1848).

44. See http://www.templeton.org/market/PDF/Bhagwati.pdf.

45. Michael Novak, "Wealth & Virtue: The Moral Case for Capitalism," speech delivered before the Mont Pelerine Society in Sri Lanka, January 11, 2004, reprinted in *National Review Online*, February 18, 2004.

46. Charles Colson and Nancy Pearcey, *How Now Shall We Live?* (Carol Stream: Tyndale House Publishers, 1999), 386.

47. Irving Kristol, *Two Cheers for Capitalism*, (New York: Basic Books, 1978), 130.

48. Luke 12:15.

49. Thomas Jefferson, "Report of the Commissioners for the University of Virginia," August 4, 1818, in *Writings*, edited by Merill D. Peterson (1984), 459.

50. See George F. Will, *Statecraft As Soulcraft: What Government Does* (New York: Simon and Schuster, 1983).

51. Peter Berger and Richard Neuhaus, *To Empower People: The Role of Mediating Structures in Public Policy* (Washington, D.C.: AEI Press, 1977).

52. William Wordsworth, *The Prelude: Book Fourteenth*, available at http://www.bartleby.com/145/ww300.html.

53. Norman Mailer, "The White Negro," in *Advertisements for Myself* (New York: Putnam, 1959).

54. Kristol, *Two Cheers for Capitalism*, 179.

55. Peter Berger, "Capitalism: The Continuing Revolution," *First Things*, November 2007.

56. See http://www.templeton.org/market/PDF/Gray.pdf.

57. Ibid.

58. Gary Becker, "How the Kibbutz and Socialism Faded Away Together," *Hoover Digest* 1 (2008).

59. Gary Becker, "The Transformation of the Kibbutz and the Rejection of Socialism," *The Becker-Posner Blog*, September 2, 2007, available at http://www.becker-posner-blog.com/archives/2007/09/the_transformat.html.

60. Ibid.

61. Tobias Buck, "The Rise of the Capitalist Kibbutz," *Financial Times*, January 25, 2010, available at http://www.ft.com/cms/s/0/01e0cdcc-09fd-11df-8b23-00144feabdc0.html.

62. Smith, *Wealth of Nations*, book X, ch. 2.

63. Jim Wallis, "The Powerful and the Powerless," in *Morality and the Marketplace*, vol. 7, edited by Michael Bauman (Hillsdale College Press), 141.

64. E. Calvin Beisner, *Prosperity and Poverty: The Compassionate Use of Resources in a World of Scarcity* (Wheaton: Crossways Books, 1988), 66.

65. Acts 4:37.

66. For more, see John Jefferson Davis, *Your Wealth in God's World: Does the Bible Support the Free Market?*, (Phillipsburg: Presbyterian and Reformed Pub Co., 1984), 81.

67. John A. Bernbaum and Simon M. Steer, *Why Work? Careers and Employment in Biblical Perspective* (Grand Rapids: Baker Book House, 1986), 6.

68. Proverbs 10:4. The great theologian Carl F.H. Henry put it this way: "Through his work, man shares the creation-purpose of God in subduing nature, whether he be a miner with dirty hands, or mechanic with greasy face, or a stenographer with stencil-smudged fingers. Work is permeated by purpose; it is intended to serve God, benefit mankind, make nature subservient to the moral program of creation. Man must therefore apply his whole being—heart and mind, as well as hand—to the daily job. As God's fellow-worker he is to reflect God's creative activity on Monday in the factory no less than on Sunday when commemorating the day of rest and worship." Quoted in Bernbaum and Steer, *Why Work?*, 6–7.

69. Michael Novak, *Catholic Social Thought and Liberal Institutions* (New Brunswick: Transaction Publishers, 2005), 221.

70. The most famous phrase in American history—"all men are created equal"—means that all people deserve equal rights. It does not mean, and it has never meant, that people are literally equal in every respect.

71. Brian Griffiths, *The Creation of Wealth: A Christian's Case for Capitalism* (Downers Grove: Intervarsity Press, 1984), 80.

72. Pope John Paul II, *Sollicitudo Rei Socialis*, December 30, 1987, available at http://www.vatican.va/holy_father/john_paul_ii/encyclicals/documents/hf_jp-ii_enc_30121987_sollicitudo-rei-socialis_en.html (accessed January 22, 2010).

73. Ibid., ch. 3.

74. Matthew 25:14–28.

75. Abraham Lincoln, speech at New Haven, Connecticut, March 6, 1860, available at http://civilwarcauses.org/newhaven.htm (accessed January 22, 2010).

76. The Homestead Act encouraged the settlement of the Western Territory by granting to each homesteader 160 acres of public land for a minimal filing fee and five years of continuous residence on that land. The Morrill Land-Grant College Act established institutions in each state to educate people in professions that were useful and practical in the mid-nineteenth century.

77. Novak, *Catholic Social Thought*, ch. 7.

78. From *Oeuvres Completes d'Alexis de Tocqueville* (Paris, 1966), 546, quoted in Friedrich A. Hayek, *The Road to Serfdom* (Chicago: University of Chicago Press, 1994).

NOTES

NOTES

NOTES

NOTES

ALSO AVAILABLE FROM COMMON SENSE CONCEPTS:

*Boom and Bust: Financial Cycles and
Human Prosperity*
by Alex J. Pollock

In *Boom and Bust: Financial Cycles and Human Prosperity*, Alex J. Pollock
argues that while economic downturns can be frightening and difficult,
people living in free market economies enjoy greater health, better access to basic necessities, better education, work less arduous jobs, and have more choices and wider horizons than people at any other point in history. This wonderful reality would not exist in the absence of financial cycles. This book explains why.

*Mere Environmentalism: A Biblical Perspective on
Humans and the Natural World*
by Steven F. Hayward

In *Mere Environmentalism: A Biblical Perspective on Humans and the Natural
World*, Steven F. Hayward provides a thorough examination of the
philosophical presuppositions underlying today's environmentalist movement and the history of policies intended to alleviate environmental challenges such as overpopulation and global warming. Relying on Scripture to understand God's created order, Hayward offers an insightful reflection on the relationship between humans and the natural world.

To order a copy of these titles or for information on how you can include
Common Sense Concepts in your classroom please visit
commonsenseconcept.com